TIME BEGINS TO HURT

Pippa Little
Time Begins to Hurt

PUBLICATIONS
2022

Published by Arc Publications,
Nanholme Mill, Shaw Wood Road
Todmorden OL14 6DA, UK
www.arcpublications.co.uk

978 1910345 28 3 (pbk)

Design by Tony Ward
Printed in Great Britain by ImprintDigital.com
Upton Pyne, Exeter, Devon

Cover illustration:
Praa Sands, Cornwall (linocut)
© Hazel McNab,
reproduced by kind permission of the artist

Arc Publications UK and Ireland Series:
Series Editor: Tony Ward

for Bob

CONTENTS

Cinderellas / 11
For Refuge / 12
the female etcetera / 13
Churchyard / 14
Snail Girl / 15
The Light and Shade Sisters / 16
Least Said / 17
Spartaca / 18
I Was So Old When I Was Not a Woman / 19
Me and Diane Arbus / 20
Coming For Our Children / 21
Inside with Full English Breakfast / 22
The Strangest Happiness / 23
Turning the Ship for Home and Then the Telling / 24
Spring Cleaning the Tigress / 25
From a Multitude / 26
Mappa Mundi / 27
Last Tractor / 28
Burned World / 29
My Son Comes to the Door / 30
West Acres / 31
Meals My Mother Made / 32
Consider the Dirt / 33
A Father Is / 34
Exit Information / 35
Mrs Red Wallpaper / 36
My Bent Corsage of You / 37
White Afternoon / 38
Grey Berber / 39
Candling / 40
The Horn Window / 41
Sticking-Place / 42
The Wife as Jug / 43
After the Last Meal / 44

A Beautiful Day to Say Goodbye / 45
Floris Candle / 46
Lighthouse and Sea Glass / 47
Europascope / 48
The First Three Words of a Wish / 49
International Friendship Museum North Korea / 50
End of Lockdown / 51
Strange Times / 52
Seven Statements / 53
After de Chirico / 54
Skunked / 56
Abject Essoldo / 57
Sparklen Bottle / 58
Isobel Gowdie / 59
My Mother's Feet / 60
'The Beginning of Love is the Eye' / 61
Last Time I See Joanna / 62
Anneal / 63
Spell for a Stonemason / 64
Oranges and Lemons / 65
The Coffin Club / 66
The Summer I Lived as a Wolf / 67
On An Extinction / 68
Gloria / 69
Time Begins to Hurt / 70
Something Is Very Wrong With Us / 71
Last Words from the Row / 72

Notes / 73
Acknowledgements / 75
Biographical Note / 77

I love you, love you, love you,
sad as you are, O world

ADÉLIA PRADO

CINDERELLAS

Tonight I am thinking about women who don't live
                                    to grow old
women barricaded in by nicotine and hair-spray's
acetone and lipstick fats,
women who don't even know they are angry.

A July night too airless for sleep
one of them sits it out in the lounge,
bad foot in its black silk slipper
propped on a stool. Smokes a cigarette

down to the filter. Hungry.
They say most of what we are
is electrical and I feel it
on nights like this.
Can blood catch fire?

Another woman who might have been my mother
flickers at the far edge of sight
like lightning or migraine,
dancing by herself.

She flew round the dark side of the moon,
returned to what possessed her.
By morning there's nothing to see
but a smirr of ashes, her throne

stripped down to its springs.
Some nights I feel my flesh
prickle and heat, as if she is
tapping at me with meaty fingers.

FOR REFUGE

Use no names. Roads
have been whited out,
redacted. Hone your oldest sense.
Learn the wind,
memorise where it goes
bearing your odours. The truck-stops
are roofless churches.
Comma-birds on power lines
swollen by rain
fall away.
Comfort yourself,
there will be stars in the dark
travelling towards you,
smaller and smaller.
Trust the earth
with your bandaged feet,
the pockets sewn shut by your mother.
Carry only such things
as snowflakes, eyelashes,
for the future may not make you out.

the woman in the wire dress / the fruit gum shoes
climbs the gallery stairs / emigrant in her life
surrounded by absent children, husbands
and versions of herself / no cloud of glory
just an unceasing buzzing of white noise /
emotional tinnitus / the gallery is cold and pale
the uniformed men bored /
she walks a centimetre or two above the ground
not enough for anyone to notice / 70 % water 30% rage /
she lists in defence two-sided things / the back of a cinema /
secretive and dirty / how dust accrues behind the sideboard
the hungry mirror, the hanged man: 'how the opposite is
                                        always true'
I woke myself up she says / *from the labours of twilight sleep*
when the lost return, how shall they look?

CHURCHYARD

Here's willow for a sailor's concern,
knuckles tapping at his mossy anchor,
the scrubbed marble doorstep
with its jar of snowdrops for an infant
unnamed and dead two lifetimes over.
I walk here all weathers, in rhododendrons'
popish purple, blackberries' wet blue
that get picked at night, in secret.
Winter now, all stab-sticks in black ground,
I've nobody here. Years ago
it was all running feet,
unearthly calls, kids in their dens
singing on glue like foxes,
but still I came anyway.
For some it's a shortcut.

SNAIL GIRL

she has gone out to look
and been missing
forty two years

coatless she ran to
where the sea grows wings
curled herself up in the pier wall
same misty colour
as wet stones and gabardine

on afternoons licked by sea and rain
invisible to most

sensitive to cold
and being odd
and being alone

THE LIGHT AND SHADE SISTERS

We held hands and held our breath,
wordless, knew what we must do
for the final show and tell before you left.
Two versions, shrunk and shadow-less,
haunt what happened next: we knew.
I held your hand, we held our breath.
A summoning for time's impress,
though Our Father said the opposite was true
that final show and tell before you left.
Likeness, unlike: stealthily, the theft.
Uneasy now to say who's who.
We held hands and held our breath.
Was his need to curse or bless?
Before the differences bled through
the final show and tell before you left
you were a safer version of myself.
He made you me, he made us two.
For the final show and tell before you left
we held hands and held our breath.

LEAST SAID

You've set a place for silence at your table,
the guest who never left, who's there
night after night at the foot of your bed,
the first thing you see every morning

and he's growing stronger. Knows his way around,
leaves the seat up, moves the clock hands forward;
as your husband pales to see-through smoke
he lounges, tanned and hefty, watching everything.

He's real, at least: nobody could accuse him
of being other than he is. Sometimes you feel
his fingers creep across your nape, his open mouth
graze yours, right under your husband's nose.

SPARTACA

in the room / in the street / on the stair / where some
men make free
in plain sight or in secret as if we were sweetmeat / to dip
fingers in and then forget – it is the being alone
afterwards that numbs and maims, being utterly
alone in the silence of it / where shame creeps in /
stuns dead / but now we rise, all of us
fondled and hurt and licked in acid jokery and hate,
pets, sweethearts, lovers, darlings, humourless bitches –
we stand together, each one a Spartaca
no longer silent or alone: each voice stronger,
massing, alive, a wild murmuration
me too   me too   me too

I WAS SO OLD WHEN I WAS NOT A WOMAN

People thought my father drank: he never said
it was my mother
who stuck like moss to dark places.
She gives us wipes for the train
to wash away the sticky fingerprints of strangers.
We descend from Ward 4 in a dark box
without him. *Street level*
says the final sign.

He is a crane-fly, hurt
and folded. He forgets
he once walked like other fathers.
I can make him strong,
afraid of nothing. That's not true.
I am ashamed for both of us.
The roads have been closed,
the railway lines pulled up.

We live and die inside these bodies.
I was so old when I was not a woman,
when I weighed nothing.

ME AND DIANE ARBUS

I'm the dwarf in high heels
somewhere in between deep shade
of that parking lot shot or the bleached drop
close-up where suicides party –

first love, she gave me man's lips
and a soul the size of The Statue of Liberty
skin-tight sateen I chose for her,
orchids spit-brown as tobacco

who'd know we had found the source of life
there on the avenue, in chance frames
at the end of a bottle's neck
and then forgotten? I loved the necklace

she made me of bites and hypos.
Ugly is not a word we recognise
she said. The flash and then the dark,
that's our country.

COMING FOR OUR CHILDREN

You worry for them
on the way to school
on the way home

how they have to cross the soldiers' path
through the rubble and rough wires
with no hiding places

one afternoon he's late,
your eight year old son
snatched by an armoured car:

the others ran away
came to tell you –
for hours you hardly breathe

don't count
each bite on your knuckle
each pace across the floor

fifteen of them surrounding him
who was throwing stones
give us their names

in his too-big spectacles
his wobbling front teeth
small and skinny

they came for him
now he never sleeps
and trembles the way you tremble

INSIDE WITH FULL ENGLISH BREAKFAST

Sun butters the bay windows of the Mermaid Café
this scorching afternoon. Outside in turquoise
blue the vista unfolds in waves –
families, dogs, parasols, the tiny lighthouse.

Inside with Full English and cappuccino
it feels like late autumn or the featureless
grey of midwinter. Not cold, just numb,
the same old weather we've brought from home.

A son sits with his father and our glances catch.
The old man nudges a screen with his pinky's knuckle.
Both have the same dreamy, absent look,
shoulders touching side by side in silence.

I am wordless too, waiting while you eat,
letting my coffee cool, watching the walkers
and paddlers in an endless, unspooling film
behind glass. We are motionless

while those other lives we lost or let go
flutter out there, moth-like in the hot light.
How strange the world's become.
I reach across the table for your hand.

THE STRANGEST HAPPINESS

Though we have no new words
for this time of illness, remission,
we go by the weight of your hand in mine,
my hand upon your shoulder

and this is the strangest happiness: no longer expecting
anything more than morning glories in the hedgerow,
birdsong,

coffee hot and strong. Some days life
feels very much the same
this way. Everything simple and separate now,

a shaft of sun across the floor. We are in love
again, and very young, and kind
with one another.

TURNING THE SHIP FOR HOME AND THEN THE TELLING

The captain's sun-sizzled, wears a cap with 'Die Trying'
stuck at an angle, fists the lumpish red of lobsters.
He's sailing the *Algetia* back from the Eastern Garbage Patch,
an unmapped country he can't board
for it jiggles and scrambles and discards itself
like knitting twirling off bone needles
but at its deep clotted heart it pulls in close,
clamps whales and crabs alike in nets and knots
and chokes – not only the lines, the ropes, the spars
but all the plastic tops and jagged fragments
whale-swallowed, a whole ocean's innards
spiked orange, fluorescent pink, green, blue –
pulled and sucked by the sea into a whorl
which grows, accrues, accumulates
hour after hour in daylight and dark,
where he is powerless except in witness,
his mourning the world takes for crazy.

SPRING CLEANING THE TIGRESS

With thanks to The National Trust Housekeeping Manual

Once you have quieted her
she will let you test for weakness.
At eyes and mouth, where skin
is thinnest, under greatest stress
along the stitching, understand
splitting may occur. Ears and tail
can tear: she is most frail
at her periphery. Still imagine
how she was when young, all
white gold and stippled darkling,
now you must do her an indignity –

the manual says damage absorbed through light,
cumulative, irreversible,
will be what does for her.
Milky-eyed behind calico blinds
she steps through unending dusk,
longs for one snarl of morning.

FROM A MULTITUDE

Words in italics taken from Engels' The Condition of the
Working-Class in England, 1844.

A person may live in it for years,
go *in and out daily,* in defiance
of the courts and lanes, pass among *covered passages,*
the shops and beer houses –

a person no more substantial to God
than a flea, inhabiting the left-behind
narrow, dirty stairs, to visit each morning
a privy without a door, step through *pools
of stagnant excrement* like a dog –

peculiarly built, this life, splintered from a *multitude* –
example of *how little space a human being
can move and breathe in,* below the bridge
where the crack dreamers dream and the drowned

lift their pale fish-smooth faces from the river's
black filth; it's that simple: the masters,
the men, the times are never changing –
one falls like a thing dead already
from *a parapet high as a man,* and is gone.

MAPPA MUNDI

It stays with me, that long-drawn-out
approaching train fattening through summer-cut fields,
the waiting for it like waiting for time to flower from its
                                        cocoon
and arrive in a fluster of smoky wings at this wall-less place
of two platforms and a cast-iron parapet's umbelliferous
                                        shadows:

I remember the drag of luggage (also how once I left with
                                        nothing)
and escaping in a slam of doors, keening whistle, the stark
                                        choice
of south or north. You, waving from the railway line.
How you shrank before I knew it, fading between fireweed
and morning glory, while I grew bigger and bigger and bigger.

LAST TRACTOR

for Beni

Dusk in October falls softly like the petals of old roses
the sky is washed warm pink
and in the dark rolling waves of the huge field
the last tractor sails, tacking to the wind
while the moon will be winsome soon
a new-boiled egg
wet and cooling to a shine.

I think of you curled and sleeping
ancient god five weeks old, someone
whose skin I don't know yet.

Seen from the farthest reaches
a glimmer of light as it is lost
turns the heart over, motor and gears,
towards you.

BURNED WORLD

Given four pandrops knotted in a hanky,
told not to go down the rutted, muddy, fox-
and tyre-imprinted track erased by rain, remade in tellings
and retellings of sweet fumes, strange goings-on, of course
we made straight for it, myself and me,
our humpbacked shadows a-spring, uncoiling
among the mossy lumber, rats' pillows' dirty plastic,
a spread feast where unseen men left
what could not catch and torched everything else
to char and ashes soft as talc: once
we curled inside a suitcase, our sprung-open nest
scorched rapture of narrow squeak, skin
of our teeth.

MY SON COMES TO THE DOOR AND WE PRACTISE SOCIAL DISTANCING

He rings to say *I'm here.*
Called ahead to ask for binbags,
labels for sorting out the house.
Everything's been left since lockdown,
suspended through these glassy days.
How long since it rained?
The sky's blue as a plate and the trees neon green
behind his unshorn head. He stands by the gate
keeping his distance. Three weeks to the day
since we last touched. Our risky hug at the funeral.

I leave what he needs on the wall,
wish I could have made him a fat iced cake,
been the kind of mother I never was.
Words are frail, moth-like, and fade
in the brightness between us.
I need to say grief is hard work
but it comes out as *go canny.*

Wanting him to stand there forever,
I want him just to go. Closing the door
I press my cheekbone hard against its inward side.

WEST ACRES

You began to trouble yourself about death
at nine years old when you would stumble
finger by finger the unlit passage to the closed door,
inch inside their smoke-fumed dark, climb them
lying back to back in bed, deliver yourself
to that scorched plain between volcanoes (one long-spent,
the other simmering): you didn't know then
being untouched was an affliction; being fed
through bars by knucklebone, you were just
ashamed of this need to return night after night
where you were made unwelcome – *too old for this*,
picked up and taken back to where death muttered
get you later from behind the curtain
and you held yourself, stoppered your mouth with your thumb
so the long smouldering-out wouldn't melt and fuse
your lungs to your spine but it would take years before
you could breathe without hurting.

MEALS MY MOTHER MADE

Mangoes ripened and fell
clotting in the tropical garden.
She'd cut them open
for me to suck their woolly flesh.
I bumbled around leaning on the dog,
mouth bright with mango glue and tongue fermenting –
but then in another country it was always grey,
the chair hard, my plate a great moon
with a secret which had to be revealed
by swallowing gristle and muscle and fat.
We'd sit there till I'd swallowed every chill bite
in the darkening room.
Those were different times.
Like the night I hadn't wanted to come home
from my friend's sweet and lawless kitchen,
told my mother I wished I wasn't hers, meaning
I hated her unhappiness
then found waiting on the night-cleared table
a special treat, spaghetti in cold cheese.
I ate it all and wanted more but couldn't ask.

CONSIDER THE DIRT

for it is a similar colour to the soles of our feet
when we began in San Pedro Sula on October 12th
the first thousand, some walking *descalzados* or
in trainers, *chanclas*, women with buggies and wheeled cases,
children on fathers' shoulders:

for it rubs raw, riddles the soft interstices of flesh -
the dirt, the earth, the quinta, the terrain, the property
pale in the heat, dark under rain:

we have become as the scum of the world,
the dregs of all things: you have made us
mere offscouring and refuse in the midst of peoples

one foot lifts, pauses while the other presses down, repeat /
                                                    repeat
for thirty miles a day, if no trucks take pity: sleep where
                                        we fall,
exhausted on the street: tomorrow, keep walking:

remembered rooms surprise us now,
for the dirt stretches away, Guatemala, Mexico, we could walk
to the end of the world with this same grit under our feet:
somebody guards every grain of it,
allows us to walk
or not: how far? So far: *stop*
but we will not stop: the dirt is naked:
like us, is commonplace and plain
and everywhere, more plentiful than lilies.

A FATHER IS

With thanks to The National Trust Housekeeping Manual

A father is a curiosity of birds' eggs
unstable in light

to be touched only with exhausted bristle
never exposed to water

a father is an antlered head
from the Tableau Hall

nostrils swabbed, eyes dusted
teeth burnished softly

a father is an old bird's nest
swelling inside the chimney

where moths will graze
and be smoked out by funnel

also a liver-pink coral
growing a starry mould under glass

a father is a death watch
that grinds through words

leaves what's left
in grey ash circles.

EXIT INFORMATION

'all the rooms we speak of are dark places'
OLIVER DE LA PAZ

You loved the story about the dark dark house
in a dark dark street where skeletons lived with smiling faces.
Someone is reading it to their child tonight

and you are grown into a stranger-man who clambered
out of the chambers of my heart for higher altitudes,
a pure light that burned the rim of the volcano.

Your brothers still talk of the dark house we hung with stars
that Christmas we chased away your love
and you left anyway. But you had been gone for years,

a sound hiding in the darkest, blindest turn of the stairs,
words embedded in a north wall. Hiding in plain sight
our loss, never spoken, always provisional

shivers like a skin-and-bone creature,
that jaunty skeleton dog in the story
who glistened white neon, grinning

as if being dead was the best stunt in the world –
bone of my bone but I am not your life's breath
and I never was. No, more than a breath, an answering.

MRS RED WALLPAPER

(chats with the Artist)

Joan, may I call you that? Far inland here
so I soak my feet in salt water,
say spells for a mermaid's tail.
Years I've been washed up in red red red
when what I want is blue, delicious, stringent.
Objects – Mother's coffee grinder, Pa's Victrola –
observe and comfort us but it's colour which saves.
I'm living inside a whale's heart, glutted crimson.
The dull thud thud thud of time… you don't hear it,
too young yet, but I see you older, facing into a gale
half in half out of the sea, as storm-spray leaps dazzling
into your oils and boat-paint, the winter inside you
                                    washed clean
day after day. I'd go there with you if I could,
into that sea-weathering of greys and greens to stone
blues, (it's how the soul fills out, is finally made visible)
but I'm growing magical myself, slowly, slowly
among my familiars of pink, crimson and cerise, so one day
you might look out to where it's deep and still and see me
coming back for you.

MY BENT CORSAGE OF YOU

for Sam, born by caesarean

Turned on my left side I was the carcass that surgeon took
                                 his knife to,
my warm salt oils gushed over the slab on to his shoes,
I liked that it made him scowl. I rolled and rolled in my
                                   mind's eye

deeper than any deep-sea creature as he began.
The gold-ringed eye is a perfect hurt, with its wet centre
one lost thing forever looking for its other. Such a long

hauling upwards from this slashed apron of fat
into grace. A queer heat hosed me down
and suddenly there was my bent corsage of you,

beached at my heart.

WHITE AFTERNOON

Join us in the garden, wind-blown
by laundry and hawthorn's steam.
Sometimes strange oppositions
between joy, say, or the old grief,
become the other. Today
is that kind of day. We are directed to be still
before the camera, and as I hold the warm
eleven months of him, he notices
a butterfly, ivory-veined, uncrumpling
against the sleeves and plackets on the line.
His obsidian eyes flash with waterfall
fire, turquoise, jade, more ancient
than my language, the paleness of me,
his stranger grandmother.

I think of marble, and snow, and many things
he's yet to see, fragile or stony, and how
long after he's gone I'll still be crazy
with love for him, how happiness burns
even as it falls away. The photograph
is taken and months from now will seem
anonymous. Rain will approach
later in a delicate stippling
and I'll run out, pull down into my arms
bundles and clouds and all my sad weather.

GREY BERBER

He thinks he's unobserved
in his lonely grace
circling the five-acre field
fence to fence –

he is a running cloud,
a fast flowing river,
ripples of mist or smoke.
I scent him on the wind,

imagine how the nap rises on his spine:
don't want to bridle
or fetter him, just watch
and watch how life

loves him whole,
muscle and bone.

CANDLING

You brought me
one for each month of her life

they lay in my palms
three small worlds

first we used a pin to prick them
I reached in with a needle

pierced the yolk and broke the membrane
but it was you

who put them to your mouth
whose lips met the paper-thin resist

bone and sorrow
and you breathed

till they were light and empty
lanterns

THE HORN WINDOW

You are yellow
as a bruised thumbnail

brimstone lingerings of smoke
or spell, smudged grains

retreating, tidal
from sky-mist, marshlands –

I kneel where the lepers knelt
at your hungry and thirsting surface

through smeary cirrus of the mind's eye
swirl of grease and holy breath,

imagine a life where we shall all be loved again
where bone meets bone and cools

deep inside the whale
I say my name

STICKING-PLACE

You said you *never asked or wanted to be born*
as if my mothering was a punishment
and the harder I loved you the more it hurt.
Things were worse once, though I refuse
to write in the past tense. And still.
You went down to the unmanned station
but no trains came. You got hit by a car
and lay in the road until I came to fetch you.
You broke glass and cried afterwards.
Weeks turned to years of few words
coming and going, my *seeing you off the premises*
a reason only to hold you for a moment.
I keep loving you like an old bruise, still tender.
You do not consider yourself *worthy of any love at all:*
I should have guarded you better from my ghosts'
white noise, their whisky breath –
I would blow fire into your mouth, set a fuse
snaking towards your heart if that would save you.
Yet the night you ran I didn't follow, part of me
relieved it might be over: when it wasn't,
I set my stubborn love at you again. Some nights
I can admit we are each other's sticking-place,
as if that could shelter us. Nothing can shelter us.
Now I listen at your door to what approaches
slowly from the dark, asking to be written.

THE WIFE AS JUG

I am unwinged.
You turn me in your hands
slippery as a newborn.
If you raised me to the air
and let me free I could not find home,
would dive to the floor
sure as flood. But my shining
offers you your Sunday face
with which you are well pleased
and serves you well. We agree, I am the weather
and the bearer of our state. If I have a flaw,
invisible, it's this: the more you fill of me,
the more hollow I become.

AFTER THE LAST MEAL

Dusk arrives shyly
so you're surprised by its frail dark
netting the high hedges,
how it deepens, pooling
in garden after garden
when you are standing at the window
rinsing cups and plates

then surprised again by the head
and shoulders of yourself
thrown as reflection by the inward
kitchen light. You are still
poised as if to disappear, but to where?
Do wild things sleepwalk,
the prick-eared lioness
with unknown distances to travel?

All along the hillside
small windows glimmer.
It might be enough that inside each
a woman paces her domain
hungry for the smell of the wind.
A solitary telephone is ringing
its closing bell as the gates shut.

A BEAUTIFUL DAY TO SAY GOODBYE

for DL

Your burial is today
my fearless and magnificent friend.
The sea-facing church shut,
only nine of us can walk with you
above the huge bay, where light's cracked and mended
wave after wave to the horizon
and Traveller piebalds graze the dunes.
No perishing wind as expected, just soft,
plum-blossom sprays
to lift our hair, a restful breathing-space in winter.

My son who loved you lowers you in,
the strap burns a slant red weal on each palm,
we mouth the only prayer, old-learned-by-heart
Forever and Ever Amen.
How you would have wanted singing.

We each come to the edge and let dry earth fall from
                                        our hands
then walk back. We are leaving you in your best shoes
and a blouse that was my Christmas present.
We don't want to go, but are told to disperse:
the gravediggers wait with masks.

FLORIS CANDLE

i.m. Bessie

The Christmas before she leaves home
I appear in the hall baring my single drop of light,
dissolve in warm oils from the south.
I disturb the cold, still air of that house
with my almost imperceptible breathing:
rosy, with undertones of musk, oud, chypre.
Though I am afraid of the dark I prefer it,
soft pressure I can push against, resist.
I rouse in her strange worlds half-formed
but the word I frame for her, in ripples
around the wick, is *go*. She doesn't know yet
how to be womanly: she will learn.
Time is falling away fine as snow.
In three winters her grandmother will be gone.

LIGHTHOUSE AND SEA GLASS

for B.

A windswept day spent at the tide's seam
diving and wading alone like sanderling
or turnstone for sea glass.

Home, I arrange my hoard on a high sill
west of the lighthouse. Dusk is setting off the beam,
slow pulse of there...*not there...*

If you were *here* would you tell me
how tumuli of spirals turn the lens to a great star
told in a rosary by sailors this long coast?

Small, tumbled things burn cold
against the window. Tell me they will abide.
Tell me they will let the young light in, come morning.

Sea-fissured, fractured smooth,
their surfaces seem to fill with tears,
mourn lost, uncrossable distance.

EUROPASCOPE

I hold you up to light
so your colours tumble, catch fire

remind me of falling in love at the lake,
lanterns strung from trees (*speckled golds, saffron,
reeds tobacco-brown*); the night we slept in a forest, cocooned
in a single sleeping bag, *owl silver, stern evergreen*
or older, on trains graffiti-slashed,
not quite visitors or guests, nor yet
inhabitants, our vowels a-swirl (*cherry black,
palinka's opalescence, coffee grounds, goldenrod*)

Here, meetings and partings with my beloveds,
my dead, bone of my bone, all fly up
and form, effortlessly, into a pure and perfect dance
(*cinnabar glow and cobalt shallows*) the day
I lay next my sister in the deep hammam of Madrid.
And long before me my elders crossed intricate borders,
pushed a thumb into bullet-holes along apartment walls
(*sorrel, bisque, according to their shadow*)
whose symmetries whirled and rushed around them
sharp-winged, indecipherable:

I hold you up to the light,
question formed from a lost question.
Either you are small, distant as a pour of stars,
or gigantic close-up of follicle, pelt;
perhaps you are only a far-away thunderstorm
(*ochre, umber*) where fine rain is falling, somewhere
I might have been born, before the lightning.

48

'THE FIRST THREE WORDS OF A WISH'

from 'Potions' by Yusef Komunyakaa

No Loitering Here, Maccy D's remind.
No cash? No warm time at the old Spot White.
The flyover splays giant fingers ringed with light,
rime seals the multi storeys. Wedding ice.
Learn to roost, bird-like, survive.
Heels ring, oaths explode, sex-echoes rise
from heated pipes. This is my life.
My life is this: or not: what spell said twice
could *skin the rabbit,* make it put right
wrongs done to me, to mine?
I wish for morning as I wish for wine,
small change to seek or heart to find.

I enter, bowing as required
before gargantuan full moons of father and son,
duly remove my shoes.
I want to learn about amity
through these tokens of esteem, parley
of giver and given-to
in these halls as big as airports,
so skim by a rubberised ashtray shaped like a missile,
Stalin's bullet-proof limo
but stop before the upright, wise-smiling crocodile
who proffers cocktails on a steel tray
for a party that never started.
He sets up a one-sided conversation
in my mother's language:
Own only what you use
for everything else, moth and rust, will return
to haunt your children.

END OF LOCKDOWN

Something has broken / been broken
in me:

today I walked where
rock pools, like eyes,
fill with tears –
alone but for gulls
and sea-glitter:

forbidden touch, skin remembers
how to hold and be held
in tenderness is holy:

the world is very old
and very frail –
I wonder / will it survive us?

Something has broken / been broken:
this slow, quiet letting go
of our pawnbroker's innocence:

I have dreamed again and again of extinction

and yet the world goes on

even as something has lain down in us
like an old animal / come to its end

multitudes throng the beaches
in these last days of lockdown
oiling their glistening legs
like flies.

STRANGE TIMES

Holy Island

If I cross the causeway
as smoulder feels its way along a fuse
will you come?

A skein's long gash
flares momentarily at dusk,
woods from the seaward side
brew warm sugars
from all that's windborne.

Dog's bark, owl's call
sadness is the must
the slow winding in

We have only skin to skin
mind to mind will to will
what else survives in the deep of cells and stars
a cold heat which at its darkest burns
old sweetnesses
for which I hungered

and still I want
want
never to die away

SEVEN STATEMENTS

He crosses out joy

he considers the Holocaust

he cuts out faces

uses their broken background.

Surgeon to the cicatrice

he works in snowfall

his Heaven is roofless.

AFTER DE CHIRICO

1. 'The Enigma of the Hour'

I am the size of my own grave.
Shadow threads me winding-clothes
with its dark needle. Brother of the red
arches, can you see it, bloodless lunar mind
approaching
with each infinitesimal steel tick
the high lunge of the hour or
the fume of a train, coming softly as war?
From the dead side, watch me, assassin,
as I watch you
from the side of the dead.

2. 'The Uncertainties of the Poet'

As a torso twisted at the hip
or noose unravelling
a train crosses this horizon:
my nib guzzles sticky, still-damp words
from its pale-skinned steam.
In a minutely different lifetime
a trick is performed backwards
(blot, black hat) and vanishes
those who should have been safe here.

3. 'The Song of Love'

A rubber red glove for a fairground heart,
the afternoon bequeathed me:
steam hammers and testifies,
testifies, but no-one is driving the train
so it neither departs nor arrives
and the sky is a midnight / midsummer
Siberia, there can be no shadows
in the imagination – what did love do
but offer eye sockets and cemented curls,
so I saw what I wanted not to see
from unglazed holes in a concrete fortress
and the trodden-under splinters
of broken-mouthed horses.

SKUNKED

for Celia

In Idaho folks forsake alcohol for speed,
chase the long featureless roads for Jesus,
break their skulls and necks with monotonous abandon.

You should see the too-late swerve,
the dent of spine on aluminium,
how the backseat upholstery

or Yamaha hubcaps come unsprung!
She drove the ambulance those years,
heard Death grind his torqued jaws,

saw skunks – not built for quick exits –
come off worst mostly, being cumbersome,
short-sighted and definitely unbiblical.

How far the lonesome speeders went
to wash their odorous damnation off!
Some nights the whole state

lapped scarlet tides, every supermart
cleared-out of tomato, fresh, canned, glassed,
in a gluttony of blood baths –

but as the sticky cure dried on flesh and wheel-well
it would always slink back, morning's
eye-watering stink, like resurrection.

She'd scrape those skunks up, each the heft
of a house cat, set them down tidy.
Wish them an afterlife, placid, pedestrian.

ABJECT ESSOLDO

after Terrance Hayes

This winter finally managed it – a bold
breach of rococo ceiling, the messy
implosion of pigeons whose sole jest
involves tidelines of milky salt
on the nap of crimson velvet seats:
they spoon sadly, these rows of rose,
love don't live here any more and the cold
performs its solitary duty: soon
where there was a jostling of bald
unready hearts, one for every ticket sold,
snow will do its old deceive, the opening solo.

SPARKLEN BOTTLE

Grandma's *sparklen*
in the winterdark house where I grew up
loved me the best:
I pushed my nose up close
to see fireflies leap and sputter,
glow-worms climb
and fall in tiny squeezes,
flayed hearts of angels –
I know she whispered
so those wandering would come
curious, too close,
then with a swift oblique
twist she'd have them
in. I like to think
it wasn't wishing
only but in the black mantle
of that house her *sparklen*
throbs still with hostage stars
and deep-sea phosphors,
tinsel glitterings of those
she couldn't kill.

ISOBEL GOWDIE

Born 1632 Auldearn

What pauses here
on long hunker-bones
listening at the eye's edge,
ferm-toun or form long gone?

From *sorrow and sych and meikle care*
slipping between worlds
at morn's blink – leap, Isobel,
headlong, sleek changeling.

MY MOTHER'S FEET

make small excursions to the garden,
cloud-soft and swollen, insteps
the shade of perished rubber,
nails smoky snail shell. Summer-bared
in Scholls they tap tap back and forward
to the drinks cabinet, the heels
and high-days long sent to Thrift.
Cupboards bulge with popsox, mink
beige and caramel, rolled up like fists.
And in another life she kicked
her two small daughters clean across the floor
then kissed them as I want to kiss her now.

'THE BEGINNING OF LOVE IS THE EYE'

'Asili ya Huba Mwanzowe ni Jicho'

I see a country whose flags are many and multi-coloured
and belong to everybody. They are ordinary and splendid
as washing, they are always speaking to one another
and asking questions. They swaddle and comfort
so you can dance in them, beat your heels, raise
your arms high, they will wrap you in life, they will sing
around you, red, yellow, emerald, crackling in the breeze.
I see a country whose every border is porous,
says *welcome, come touch, come in.*
Imagine such a country!
Then suddenly it's here
in Lubaina's afternoon
as a flowering of freed children rush
through, among, between the banners,
pull on the red ropes to re-arrange her dreams
into their own.

it's a pouring afternoon, she's winding wool in a loose, elongated loop while the ball, fern green, fattens in her lap. We take turns stretching the soft spool between us, smoothing snags while our talking lifts, falls, gathers. Under the aquatic light from the glass roof her long hair gleams and is beautiful. Each visit she's somewhere farther out, beyond my following, yet we can talk about anything. She tells me of old friends, their gift of Sarah Ravens tulips; remembers the bulbs' weight within their rustle of brown paper, years' worth of blooms promised inside each one. How the presence of women's friendship, quieter than family and men-folk, seems urgent now, important. Ten days later I'll come to her funeral without a coat, stand afterwards in the churchyard among white crocus quills, alone, and overhear a woman say *we opened our hearts to each other* so for a moment my heart flares – she was *my* friend – before I feel the pull, again, the good suppleness of green between her hands and my own.

ANNEAL

I would bring you the quartz-scribbled stone
from the last walk on the beach, and the thermos of sweet coffee
shared watching waves crumple from the warmth of the car:
I would bring you newspaper puzzles and old war films,
small rituals of touch and watching together for wild birds,
the calendar and alarm clock, green jacket and stick,
the soft plush dressing gown in kingfisher blue, the shoes
no longer worn, the slow slipping away, the shifting of light,
the waiting: all these I would arrange with infinite care
before you as if you could bless them
as molten glass a moment before the anneal
when it might become anything.

SPELL FOR A STONEMASON

for Ken

She flies far south for a day and a night,
a night and a day.

This first early dusk
we are turning away from the sun:

I stir cumin, turmeric and saffron into burnished oil
as god-speed and in gratitude for soon

your hands will remember how cut stone sings with cold,
new tombs memorise themselves in frost.

Last night you brought it, gold leaf fine as skin
for the bleached sockets of her boy's name

on his wind-scoured grave. It warms itself now
in the ammonite darkness of her case.

My kitchen's yellow-deep, rich as a Velásquez.
I think how loving kindness can anneal old hurts,

bless dry tributaries; how my spoon's arc,
swirling trails of gleam and solder,

is a kind of wildfire
seen from a back road far into the woods.

ORANGES AND LEMONS

for AC

I still have her Chinatown cleaver
from that summer she researched the history of rape
and cooked furiously every night while growing thinner.

Beast of a thing, it left metallic residue on the palm
bitter as aspirin. Inner city sirens called rioters to prayer,
helicopter searchlights kept laddering our dark.

Distracting nursery rhymes, so queerly British,
didn't do the job. *Here is a candle to light you to bed /
here is a chopper to chop off your head.*

After she left, I hid it and forgot. Now found by chance
I heft it from hand to hand: how dank and dull
the rust-flecked blade has grown:

chicken-feet scrape and catch again in my throat,
her *chop / chop / chop* gathers speed like a train,
dark and light, passing through, passing for

facts that night after night
I refused to face:
even now, none of us are safe.

THE COFFIN CLUB

Happy afternoons under the tin roof of HQ,
sanding and sawing the ta-ra-boom-de-ay of our hearts.
Dowels, end-grain and radiata pine delight us,
surfaces release top-notes of forest
charged with our hands' sweat. We've been made
strong again by these 'joyful epitaphs
in wood'. Handles get tapped in, Brasso-ed,
then last of all we fetch and fold
family linens, hand-sewn, heirloom,
so lying down to rest will smell of home.

The radio plays *Cuando Cuando Cuando,*
it's time to fill Brown Betty, catch up on chat
and ailments: today there's another gap around our table
but soon everything we love will be all around us.

THE SUMMER I LIVED AS A WOLF

I knew the names of stones at the river mouth
crossed giving thanks to their uneasy spirits

I heard killings in the shadows, knew to turn keen and quick,
travel in the presence of thunder, leave no scent or spoor behind.

Preferring the high places closest to the moon
where the wind ran with me, I practised abandon,

my spine a scimitar, star-whetted, flayed old disguises
into strands and rips: underneath I was sleek, open:

my muzzle carved air into four queendoms and I knew them all
as they knew me, tooth, soul, tatterdemalion heart

and I flew, I think, in that time, when nobody needed
or shamed me and I was always hungry, bloody-tongued

but louche and free and supple, perfumed in pine and ashes.

ON AN EXTINCTION

for Great-Uncle John William Barrie Fenton

All that falls to earth, the earth undoes.
What speaks, speaks through touch:
some of us lie deep but
retrieve ourselves at last:
a bruise of soft brown rose
long after the hand left the cheek
or the fist, the wall.
All that cannot splinter, cannot mend
goes along with us,
some *fall through cracks*:
I am looking at this image of a grave
in a Toronto suburb: cheap slab,
unruly weeds, *Rest in Peace*.
Someone we never knew,
banished, erased in whispers,
shadow overlapping shadow.

GLORIA

How will they look back, the boys,
once I'm very far away but waving
from the car-boot field of afterlife,
matrioshka of woolly hats, poems,
tea-stained postcards, teapots,
songs with maudlin refrains?

Heaven may well be a table wonky from wallpapering,
bearing up against assortments random yet ordained:
it may, on the other hand, be a dismal place
where everything's 'laid out nice' and nothing's framed;
that old slipstream *life*
sucks at my sons now, birls them along:
they are men, men, men.
I'm not a snail, shell within shell
that can lick up its own sticky track
to reveal myself among the gallimaufry
in plain sight – where they might almost see me.

Rain starts to fall. Somewhere else
in a different lifetime
another table's set, bread cut
with a blunt knife, curtains shut
against the broken-hearted calling
still stuck in my chest.
Who was I to them?
Who was I to myself?

TIME BEGINS TO HURT

I love how, lying in bed behind yellow curtains
under an open window, a dog barks
somewhere in the neighbourhood,
a dog I may know from morning walks
or not – and the sound carries then fades
as evening turns towards dark: a door shuts,
the dog's gone in, all of us safe
in this small place surrounded by beeches,
under our own rooftops:

I love how rain falls in the early hours
across the streets, steady pulse
like a runner in plimsolls alone out there,
someone young and fleet making for that door
before the key turns, the hall light goes out:
keep running, keep running, my heart blurts,
you are so near now in your shining skin,
phone wires across the yards begin to warm
and thrum in sympathy, I lie with my life
waiting as always for morning on my chair,
a shapeless thing, nothing in its pockets.

SOMETHING IS VERY WRONG WITH US

Humans are 0.01% of the living, murderers of 83% of wild mammals

this fire and flood summer
it oozes out of the earth
dull throb of knowing

and seventeen days and nights orca has carried her
                                       newborn dead
photographed / filmed / followed / for a thousand miles

I walk back and forth at the edge of this northern sea
can't leave can't rest

with no language to say this in any other way
sea calls, repeats   *the harm / the damage*

two lost before this one which she won't let go
constantly retrieving and lifting its sinking body
pushing against the will of the sea
how her body trembles   I dream of the weight   the cold throat
closing up in silence again and again

bloodsong   bloodcall   *the hurt / the damage*

this evening a report   six females circle her
close and slow
she has allowed her young to slip away
fall through the soft layers and threads of the sea

and who will mourn us twelve generations from now,
mourn the tar sands, the pipelines,
the fish-greed farms,
the harm / the damage?

71

LAST WORDS FROM THE ROW

everybody has been so good to me
I'm going to heaven
see you when I get there

most of the time
I'm alone
life is short,
we don't have to kill one another

'Cinderellas' p. 11

In 1951 Mary Hardy Reeser died aged 67 apparently of Spontaneous Human Combustion. The *Minneapolis Star* named her 'The Cinder Lady'.

'The Light and Shade Sisters' p. 16

'for holding a séance there must be a minimum of at least three people present' from *Instructions in the Occult*, 1917.

'Coming for Our Children' p. 21

For Ibitha Ayash whose son Obeida was taken from his neighbourhood in West Jerusalem and interrogated by the Israeli Border Police.

'Consider the Dirt' p. 33

On July 12 2018 a procession of people left violence and poverty in Honduras, Nicaragua and Guatemala to walk to the USA and claim asylum. The 'migrant caravan', as it was called, swelled to over 5000 men, women and children. In January 2019 authorities contained many of them at the Mexican / US border.

Descalzados: barefoot *chanclas*: flip flops

'We have become the scum of the earth...' from I Corinthians 4:13

'Mrs Red Wallpaper' p. 36

'Mrs Red Wallpaper' Joan Eardley, 1949, Oil on canvas, Castlegate House Gallery, Cockermouth.

The poem imagines the sitter talking to Joan Eardley who was then 25.

'Sparklen Bottle' p. 58

('sparklen' Middle English: also 'sparken', to spark)

'International Friendship Museum North Korea' p. 50

From a photograph in the Mary Evans Picture Library.

'The Beginning of Love is the Eye' p. 61

Lubaina Himid's exhibition 'Our Kisses Are Petals', part of 'Raising the Flag' at the Baltic Centre for Contemporary Art, Gateshead, in 2018, used lengths of Swahili text kanga cloth decorated with her designs which could be re-arranged as flags by visitors.

'Isobel Gowdie' p. 59

Left a dictated 'confession' of witchcraft, including shape-shifting into hares.

'The Coffin Club' p. 66

Motto of the club, Rotorua, NZ: 'It's A Box Until There's Someone In It'. The elderly learn carpentry as community support and to save funeral expenses.

'Last Words from the Row' p. 72

Words in italics are from 'Last Words of Prisoners Before Execution'. *tgcj.texas.gov.*

Other words are taken from an interview with executioner Jerry Givens who became an anti-death penalty activist. *The Guardian,* 21 Nov 2013.

ACKNOWLEDGEMENTS

Acknowledgements are due to the editors of the following print and online publications and sites in which some of these poems first appeared: *Acumen, Aiblins, Agenda* 'All Becomes Art Part 1', *Atrium, Beautiful Dragons, Butcher's Dog, Carers UK Anthology 2020*, Maria Isakova Bennett's *Coast to Coast to Coast*, Richard Skinner's *14, Ghost Fishing* ed. Camille Dungy, Helen Ivory's *inksweatandtears*, Peter Robertson's *interlitq*, Mark Ulyseas' *Live Encounters, Magma, #MeToo Anthology, MsLexia,* Hugh McMillan's *Plague Poems / Poems from the Backroom* and *Dead Guid Scots*, Roncadora Press, Bill Herbert & Andy Jackson's *Postcards from Malthusia, POETRY, Poetry Ireland Review, The Compass, The Lit Quarterly, The Manhattan Review, The Rialto, The Stinging Fly, The Moth,* Carol Ann Duffy's *WRITE Where We Are NOW, The Poetry Archive, Mary Evans Picture Library, Dark Mountain* 19.

'Europascope' won first prize in A Poem for Europe 2020. 'The Strangest Happiness' won the inaugural Aryamati Prize in 2020. 'Inside With Full English Breakfast' won first prize in the Carers UK Poetry Competition 2020. 'White Afternoon' won second prize in the Second Light Poetry Competition 2019.

I would like to thank Jo Clement, Suzannah V. Evans, Jack Little and Paul Batchelor for their support, Hazel McNab for her beautiful print 'Praa Sands', The Royal Literary Fund, Women Poets' Workshop at Newcastle University, Carte Blanche, Jane Marshall, Geraldine Green, all the editors to whom I've submitted poems, my friends and, always, my family.

BIOGRPAHICAL NOTE

PIPPA LITTLE is Scots but has settled in the North East of England where she cared for her husband until his death in 2020. She devised and delivered pilot workshop programmes on expressive writing for first year students at Newcastle University through the Royal Literary Fund. Since becoming involved with conservation projects and supporting migrants and asylum seekers, particularly unaccompanied children, these concerns have increasingly informed her writing.